Attraction Marketing Techniques

How to Make Customers Find and Buy from Your Business

Sarah Carter

Copyright © 2020 Hook Heath Publishing
www.hookheathpublishing.com

About the Author – Sarah Carter

 An ex-model that went on to become a successful freelance consultant in the financial services industry.

The books are based on the techniques used over the years in business working as a consultant.

It is deliberate the books are not too long, but sufficient to give you a background into the subject. After all, 'Brevity is the soul of wit', William Shakespeare.

Whether you are an author or have worked in financial services, I'd love to your story. My email is Sarah@hookheathpublishing.com

Contents

About the Author – Sarah Carter 3
Contents 5
About Attraction Marketing 7
The Basics 8
Does Attraction Marketing really work? 10
How to Apply Attraction Marketing 12
Part 1: Consumers Find You 13
Website Design First 13
Article Directories 14
Social Networking Websites 16
Step 1 – Why is Building a Network So Important? ... 20
Step 3 – Provide Information to Potential Customers . 27
Informational, Not Spam 28
Develop A Plan 29
Constructing Emails 30

About Attraction Marketing

Attraction marketing is a technique used by many Internet Marketers. It is rapidly becoming a highly profitable and important marketing technique that is low cost but very effective.

This book will help you understand what it is, how it is used and how it can be used in your own online business. It works with virtually every type of online business sector or niche.

When applied correctly it is a very powerful marketing tool.

The Basics

In simple terms, Internet marketers use attraction marketing to attract customers to their online business.

Attraction marketing is about customers coming to you rather than the business owner going after new clients.

This compares to the traditional technique for print based or off line advertisings where business owners spend significantly more money trying to find customers that would be interested in their product or service.

For example, advertising posters placed by the roadside or in public places like railway stations.

Such advertising is targeted at customers most likely to use the product or service rather than the customer coming directly to the provider.

This compares to attraction marketing, where the customer comes directly to your business because they have noticed the product or service may be if interest.

Therefore, this customer is presented with advertisements in a friendly format. Internet marketing is a technique of providing information to customers who are already interested in the product or service.

This can you're your business grow quickly using attraction marketing.

Does Attraction Marketing really work?

The short answer to this question is yes. There are plenty of great examples of how it has been used effectively.

One good one is to consider the election of President Obama is the United States. According to many professionals, whoever the American citizens were voting for it was clear the ability to use Internet marketing, including attraction marketing methods, helped him win him the election as President.

Internet marketing techniques were used as his campaign team knew the importance and success it could achieve.
In today's culture, people all around the word use the internet to find the information they require.

Furthermore, the Internet provides a simple and efficient resource to reach a large audience every day. This had not previously been possible before the Internet.

Attraction marketing was used to win the Presidential Election of the United States. Using attraction marketing tools, websites, and even resources like Google Ads helped him to success.

Twitter.com was used by the President as one of the many methods of attraction marketing. He gathered a huge following on the platform and communicated with short video clips. He could communicate with everyday people, put his message out and do it all without spending a penny.

Another example of this is Facebook.com. Everyone knows the younger generation use the platform to find people and chat. In fact, businesses, politicians, and even employers are using it as a tool to connect with others. The President's Facebook page was another use of attraction marketing that helped him to get his message across.

How to Apply Attraction Marketing

There are three main components to building a successful attraction marketing campaign, Any Internet marketer can apply these techniques to their own Internet business. And the good news is that none of them are time consuming, difficult, costly.

In short, the three main components are as follows:

1) Potential Consumers find you, your products or services on the internet.

2) Consumers give you permission to communicate them via the web.

3) You provide consumers with information that is of use and be valuable to them through email or social media platforms to give you a competitive advantage.

These concepts are explained in detail below.

Part 1: Consumers Find You

Attraction marketing means the customer is coming to you. The first step in the process is to get people to find you online. You are not advertising directly or going out searching for customers. So, how do you get people to find you online?

Website Design First

There are several ways to enable more customers to find you.

The ideal first step is to have a useful website or blog where you can interact with your visitors.

It is important content information based rather than sales orientated. Attraction marketing is far more likely to work than online, sales gimmicks, long sized sales letters.

Your website should feel visitors that are being provided with a service or information and not a sales ad to convince them to make a purchase.

Article Directories

You can prepare excellent articles to help get your information to your customers. These articles can be posted in multiple article directories.

There are two main benefits of this approach. Due to the popularity of many of these websites, Google ranks articles quickly and many get first page of Google results if they are correctly optimized. Therefore, when a customer is looking for information on your product or service, they are more likely to find you quickly via Google.

The purpose of article directories is to allow website owners to use such articles (providing they keep your details in the including your details in the article) and use them in websites or blogs. Their readers instantly get to read your information and can click on the link and take them back to your website to make a purchase.

Such articles also provide useful backlinks to your website which can be a boost to the Google ranking of your own website. ranking in Google and other search engines. The more back links pointing into your website, the more people will find your website. And, all you have done is write an article.

Social Networking Websites

There are various additional methods to consider for attraction marketing techniques. Social Network websites are a very popular method to obtain additional exposure for your business. Social networking is a method of gaining exposure to other people on your chosen subject matter.

Social networking websites were rarely design to help business owners market their business. However, many of these websites can be used for this purpose. Furthermore, many politicians and celebrities also use social networks to communicate with their target audience.

The social network websites are a great way to communicate and deliver your message and deliver information to your target audience. On receipt of the information they can then get in touch with your business to help deliver their requirements. The approach is used in virtually every type of business.

Below are some examples of Social networking websites than can be used in this way:

- Digg.com
  Provides articles and blog postings to your target audience. Dig provides a concept known as a Digg. A Digg is basically a vote to approve the article or

  post. The more people Digg the content, the more others will review the article or bog post. The articles can also provide links back to your website thus generating viewers of your website content.

- StumbleUpon
  Provides a similar concept to Digg allowing users to review your Articles as they 'Stumble Upon Them'

- Facebook.com
  Is arguable one of the most popular Social Networking websites for meeting new people, socialising and providing content about yourself, your business or virtually

anything else. It allows people to connect with each other and Like or Share their content.

- MySpace.com
Allows people to share information, connect and network with other users and direct people back to your website.

- YouTube.com
An ideal website to share information in the form of video content. The website can be used to promote your business and deliver your message.

- Twitter.com
Allows users to share brief messages and provide links back y other content or your website. It allows users to keep their followers updated with new information, network and develop your target audience. The website is very popular and many followers to review your content many times per day.

These are just a few examples and there many more similar websites that can be used to share your information. The ideal approach is to try multiple websites and establish which work best for delivering your message.

The key is providing regular up to date and useful content to obtain the best results.

Other popular Social Networking Websites include:

- Instagram
- LinkedIn
- Quora
- Reddit

The use of Social Networking Websites, so the best approach is to find a few that work best for your purpose.

Step 1 – Why is Building a Network So Important?

Building a Network is so important for successful Attraction Marketing. However, it is often a step that is overlooked causing the approach to be less successful than desired.

As an example, when building a following on Facebook, if you add a few pictures and your contact details, but do little else. There is little on the page for you to help you explain to you can help your followers through your business.

In order for Attraction Marketing to work, you need to build a large network of followers by providing regular and useful information. For example, you create a login at Digg.com, a social networking website that works quite indirectly for getting visitors to websites.

Tracking results is key to make the best use of your time.

If you discover that posting to certain social networks does not generate much traffic or interest, it might be worth considering alternative websites.

You need to be active and make use of your Network. Many will draft a schedule to track when to post to websites and track the results of each post. You should also consider posting on different days of the week and different times of the day to see which posts get the best results.

Below are a few suggestions to make the most of your network:

- Add a much detail to your profile
Your user profile is an important factor in getting people to visit your website. The profile should include keywords associated with your business, but in an informal but discreet way. You should not use you user profile as a sales pitch.

- Socialise with others
Look for other people on websites that share common interests and add them to your network. As an example, if you were promoting baby products and you are a mother, promote yourself as a mother first, connecting with other mothers.

- Build a network from your friend's networks Look to see if any friends are users of your favourite social network websites and add them to your network. You can also go further and see who they are connected to and make contact with them in your network. This is not just a on off exercise, so keep looking for new people to add to your network.

- Keep building your social network and try to enjoy the process. This will enable others to find out about you and visit your website and find out what you can offer that may be of interest. That may they might be more likely to buy the product or service you have to offer. This is proven as a successful process and attracts people to you without you saying too much about your business.

Step 2 – Ask for Approval to Connect.

An important part of Attraction Marketing is gaining approval to from people to allow you to communicate with them through your network. This is an important step, particularly as legislation develops regarding spam content and other inappropriate Communication. Therefore, it is essential for Internet Marketers to stay compliant with this legislation. Inappropriate communication is likely to lead to complaint and may lead to you being banned from using a particular website.

In order to market your business to your network, you therefore need to have approval to communicate with potential customers, clients or website visitors to send them any form of communication unless it is communication via a blog posting or article.

To be successful in Internet Marketing, your need this approval to get your product or service visible to your network. This is an essential part of your sales process.

This can be achieved in many ways but is an essential part of Attraction Marketing. You want attract your network to visit your website and ideally sign up to your mailing list. This is one way of obtaining permission to send them more information.

Getting people to sign up to your website involves the use of lead capture software. Some popular tools include Get Response and Aweber. Alternatively, you can create your own lead capture pages.

There are four key steps in the lead capture process:

- People discover your information on websites

- Individuals follow the links to the lead capture page on your website

- They enter their contact details on your lead capture page.

- You then have a potential lead with their permission communicate, provide information or sell your product or service.

Step 3 – Provide Information to Potential Customers

Even after going through this process, you still may not have made a profit.

The final part of the three-step process of Attraction Marketing is required.

The contact details you have gathered are then used to promote your product or service so you can generate a profit.

Although the process may seem like hard work and log, you are going to automate the process. Furthermore, you are going to do all three steps at the same time so you are likely to start making money from attraction marketing right from the beginning of the process.

Informational, Not Spam

A key factor in building a successful Attraction Marketing plan is not to be overly sales like. You need to provide information to the client. This is not about hard selling your product or service. Hence the name Attraction Marketing. The customer is attracted to you because you are giving them valuable information and tools to use.

Remember, focus on providing valuable information, not sales ads.

Develop A Plan

You will need a plan as to how you will use the authority given to you by the customer who visited your website,

The plan needs to be very specific. You have their consent to send them information in the form of emails. The customers who are on your list allow you to contact them again with more valuable information.

The plan enables you to get people to your website in a professional manner.

You plan to attract people to your website by first telling them something valuable. The visitor needs to feel they are receiving what they expected. Only in this way will they make a purchase from you.

Therefore, any communication needs to be relevant and appreciated and the customer has the best information. That way they are most likely to visit your website.

Constructing Emails

Produce a newsletter or other email communication that contains quality content to your readers. Below are some examples of what to include in the communication:

- Include Informational Articles
  Provide your readers with content they will want to receive that provides value. Customers want to read something that teaches them something. As an example, if you are selling a product on acne, the email message to your readers may explain what causes acne. This provides them with useful information.

- Make the most of the email subject line
  One of the most common mistakes is that many people have when using any form of email marketing is not getting readers to open the email. Therefore,

always use your subject line to attract people to open the email.

· Personalise the email
If you have ever opened up an email and read it knowing that they were just selling something. You should include reader's name and make sure to address it to them. Be personal, yet also professional.

· Keep images to a minimum
Don't include too many images in email marketing. You have very little time to impress the reader and you want them to read the email. Too many images mean the email will take too long to open, the reader may close the email before actually reading what you have to say.

· Instruct the reader what to do next
Make sure the reader responds to the email how in the way you planned. Tell

the reader what to do or what they can do to learn more. Provide a link to follow that takes them to the answers to their questions.

Attraction marketing is only as good as the information you provide. Therefore, take the time make it as good as possible.

Below are some more ideas for your emails:

- Be passionate about the information you are providing in the emails that is useful and relevant.

- Share details of a good book or informational product that in some way relates to your business indirectly.

- Provide details of live event information. Perhaps you are offering a live seminar or webinar. Invite your readers to visit your website if they want to attend.

- Perhaps you are offering a special offer and you want to provide details to the reader.

- Maybe you are providing some training material or video and want to share the details with your list.

Hopefully this provides some ideas of that to include in your emails.

The campaign should get people back to your website and take the action you desire.

There are many ways Attraction Marketing can be used to generate more sales for your business.

Make the effort to incorporate Attraction Marketing in your campaign and traffic will come to your website from many sources.

You will to see your sales increase providing have given the reader the helpful information to make take the desired action.

Invest the time to get quality traffic to your website.

www.ingramcontent.com/pod-product-compliance
Lightning Source LLC
Chambersburg PA
CBHW030549220526

45463CB00007B/3037